# CREEPY CRAWLY INSECTS: 1ST GRADE SCIENCE WORKBOOK SERIES

SPEEDY
PUBLISHING

Speedy Publishing LLC
40 E. Main St. #1156
Newark, DE 19711
www.speedypublishing.com

Insect bodies have
three parts, the thorax,
abdomen and head.

Bullet ant, named on account of its powerful and potent sting due to its venom. A sting from just one of them is compared to being shot with a bullet.

Earwigs feed on leaves, flowers, fruits, mold and insects. Earwigs get its name due to the myth that they crawl into your ear if you slept on the ground.

Wheel bug is one of the largest terrestrial true bugs in North America. Wheel bug attacks its prey with vicious stabbing motions using the fang at the front of its head.

Giant burrowing cockroach is the largest cockroach in the world. They are native to Australia and mostly found in tropical parts of Queensland.

Silverfish is a
small, wingless
insect. Silverfish
have inhabited
this planet
for over 400
million years.

Termites build big colonies. Each colony can have millions of members. Termites play a vital role in the ecosystem by recycling waste material such as dead wood, feces and plants.

Tarantula hawk wasp is found across most of the Southwest down into Mexico. Their sting is considered the second most painful insect sting in the world.